LEARNING
ON THE SCHOOL BUS

LEARNING
ON THE SCHOOL BUS

*A Reading Comprehension and Creative Writing Workbook
for Secondary Students*

Keshia L. Gaines, Ph.D.

Learning on the School Bus
A Reading Comprehension and Creative Writing Workbook
for Secondary Students

iUniverse books may be ordered through booksellers or by contacting:

iUniverse LLC
1663 Liberty Drive
Bloomington, IN 47403
www.iuniverse.com
1-800-Authors (1-800-288-4677)

Because of the dynamic nature of the Internet, any web addresses or links contained in this book may have changed since publication and may no longer be valid. The views expressed in this work are solely those of the author and do not necessarily reflect the views of the publisher, and the publisher hereby disclaims any responsibility for them.

Any people depicted in stock imagery provided by Thinkstock are models, and such images are being used for illustrative purposes only.
Certain stock imagery © Thinkstock.

ISBN: 978-1-4917-1135-4 (sc)
ISBN: 978-1-4917-1136-1 (e)

Printed in the United States of America.

iUniverse rev. date: 09/23/2014

TABLE OF CONTENTS

(3.) Chapter 3: The School Bus: A Yellow Classroom

(4.) Chapter 4: The Cafeteria: Academics for Breakfast and Lunch

(5.) Chapter 5: The Bathroom: An Independent Study and Other Controversial Areas to Learn

(6.) Chapter 6: The Playground: A Fun Place to Learn

PREFACE

Dear Student(s),

This workbook is designed to show you fun, creative, and unique ways to learn outside the classroom. It is a student version of my book *Why are Students Not Learning on the School Bus?* Most of you are not exposed to academic content outside the classroom very often. However, these out-of-the-classroom areas can positively influence student learning. Why are most students not learning at the bus stop, school bus, cafeteria, bathrooms, hallways, playgrounds, and from educational clothing? As a secondary student, you will write about, create methods, and complete activities about learning in unique areas. I hope you enjoy this workbook and consider all methods and areas as places for learning opportunities.

-Keshia L. Gaines, Ph.D.

About the Book

Learning on the School Bus: A Reading Comprehension and Creative Writing Workbook for Secondary Students

provides unique opportunities for teaching students about learning outside the classroom. The author, Keshia L. Gaines, Ph.D., offers ground-breaking techniques to expand areas for learning opportunities. Research has shown that academic achievement is related to the amount of time a student is engaged in learning. During the school day, missed learning opportunities occur during transition times, bathroom breaks, intercom interruptions, lunch time, and many other unstructured and unplanned times. The author's new "Bus-stop 2 Bus-stop™" method is designed to replace non-academic times with unique learning opportunities for outside the classroom. (When this workbook refers to "learning on the school bus" or "learning outside the classroom," the author is referring to learning academic content).

Audience and Purpose

This workbook is designed for use by students in various secondary classrooms and for general use by anyone who would like to complete writing activities and create new methods for learning outside the classroom. The chapters provide insight to new ways for improving academic achievement in America. *Learning on the School Bus* is also appropriate for other academic courses because of its discussion questions, higher depth of knowledge activities, and critical thinking areas. The purpose of this workbook is to explain the "Bus-stop 2 Bus-stop™" learning method and to ultimately improve the current education system in America. Also, this workbook's purpose is to provide students with an interesting and educational learning experience.

Goals and Features of this Book

There are three goals of this workbook.

1. To provide students with unique creative writing and learning opportunities
2. To increase student awareness of the new "Bus-stop 2 Bus-stop™" learning method
3. To explain new methods and areas for students to learn outside the classroom

Also, this workbook can help students learn ways to take responsibility for their own education. In order to meet the above goals, this workbook includes discussion questions, journal activities, informative graphics, vocabulary words, and more. These are great tools to initiate student group discussions and unique school projects.

The vocabulary words from each chapter's word review will be in bold lettering once within the chapter. In addition, a few QR Codes (Quick Response Codes) will be featured throughout the book. These QR Codes will take you directly to a web page when scanned by a smartphone with a QR Code app. For practice, scan the QR Code below to read an article about "learning on the school bus."

Content and Organization

"Learning on the School Bus" consists of seven chapters. The following outline highlights the seven chapters in a brief summary:

1. **Chapter 1:** Introduction to the new "Bus-stop 2 Bus-stop™" Learning Method—This chapter introduces the new "Bus-stop 2 Bus-stop™" areas for learning outside the classroom. It also gives a general overview, the author's beliefs, and a veteran teacher's perspective on learning outside the classroom.

2. **Chapter 2:** The Bus Stop: The First Area for Learning— This chapter explains why the bus stop should be the first area for students to get exposure to academic content.

3. **Chapter 3:** The School Bus: A Yellow Classroom— Chapter 3 describes the learning opportunities that can take place on a school bus. Also, the author shares her invention, The Universal School Bus Seat Learning Pad, as one of the first devices to promote student learning on the school bus.

4. **Chapter 4**: The Cafeteria: Academics for Breakfast and Lunch—This chapter was inspired by the author's 130 page dissertation titled *A Quantitative Study of Learning in the School Cafeteria Using Educational Placemats*. It explains how learning opportunities for students can be utilized during breakfast and lunch time.

5. **Chapter 5:** The Bathroom: An Independent Study— and other controversial areas to learn. This chapter

discusses how to turn the school's bathroom, a commonly low supervised area of the school, into a brief learning opportunity. In addition, this chapter discusses other controversial and unique areas for students to learn.

6. **Chapter 6:** The Playground: A Fun Place to Learn—Even though there are many hidden academic learning activities on the school playground, often times they are not maximized. The author explains fun ways for students to learn while playing.

7. **Chapter 7:** Bus-stop 2 Bus-stop™ Educational Clothing for Faculty, Staff, and Students—This chapter incorporates school culture, fashion, and learning content on clothing as a visual aid.

Special Thanks

"First, I would like to thank God for giving me the strength and the ability to be successful in my research and book writing endeavors. Also, I am thankful to God for allowing me to create the Bus-stop 2 Bus-stop™ learning method. I hope this method is a blessing to schools across the United States of America and other parts of the world. In addition, I would like to thank my husband and wonderful family for supporting me over the years. Last but not least, I dedicate this workbook to all K-12 students across the United States of America."

"Also, I would like to thank all crossing guards, bus drivers, security guards, cafeteria staff, janitorial and maintenance staff, secretaries, and other nonacademic school personnel.

You play a very important role in your school's culture. In the future, you will help students even more by increasing their academic achievement by non-traditional methods. I sincerely thank you."—Dr. Gaines

Acknowledgements

The author would like to acknowledge and show appreciation to Mrs. Rachel Taylor of Westminster, South Carolina for her editing services on *Learning on the School Bus: A Reading Comprehension and Creative Writing Workbook for Secondary Students.* As Development Editor, Mrs. Taylor worked closely with Dr. Keshia L. Gaines to edit and revise this workbook. As well, Dr. Gaines would like to say a special thank you to Mrs. Stacy Jinkins of Sorrento, Florida for her assistance with select photo-editing and graphics throughout the book.

Bus-stop 2 Bus-stop, LLC

ABOUT THE AUTHOR

Keshia L. Gaines, Ph.D.

Keshia L. Gaines, Ph.D. is an internationally recognized author, educator, and inventor in the areas of education and nontraditional learning methods. Dr. Gaines has been active in public education for over 10 years. As a young educator, Gaines works hard to create innovative methods for increasing student achievement. Dr. Gaines is the founder of Bus-stop 2 Bus-stop, LLC, a company that specializes in educational books, products, clothing, and services.

The academic background of Dr. Gaines includes a Bachelors of Arts (B.A.) in English from The University of Southern Mississippi, a Masters in Education (M.Ed.) from William Carey College, and a Doctorate of Philosophy (Ph.D.) in Educational Leadership from The University of Southern Mississippi.

Gaines has worked with elementary, middle school, and high school students in several school districts. Her experience includes teaching both general education and exceptional education students. Currently, she holds a MS Educator License with endorsements in Art, Elementary Education, English, Exceptional Education, Library Media Specialist, and School Administration.

Dr. Gaines is a native of Mississippi. She enjoys traveling and spending time with her husband Kevin Gaines, a successful business manager, and close family and friends. For further information on Bus-stop 2 Bus-stop, LLC or Dr. Gaines go to www.BusStop2BusStop.com.

CHAPTER 1

Introduction to the Bus-stop 2 Bus-stop™ Learning Method

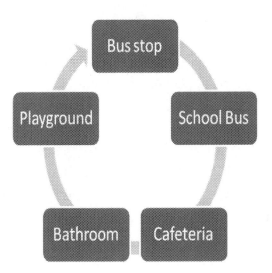

Bus-stop 2 Bus-stop™—a learning method for increasing academic achievement by exposing students to academic content outside the classroom (areas such as the bus stop, school bus, cafeteria, bathrooms, hallways, playgrounds, other school areas, and by academic content on clothing of all students and staff members). The Bus-stop 2 Bus-stop™ Learning Method was created by Dr. Keshia L. Gaines in the Fall of 2010.

As a result of the Bus-stop 2 Bus-stop™ learning method, Dr. Gaines founded Bus-stop 2 Bus-stop, LLC, a company that specializes in educational books, clothing, products, and services.

Why are students not learning outside the classroom?

Since students are not meeting academic expectations in the general classroom, it is important to consider all available nontraditional areas and methods for students to learn. Learning outside the classroom can and will make a **significant** improvement in academic achievement if opportunities are introduced and **implemented** properly. This is heavily supported by current and past research. Researchers and practitioners have identified the need to develop **alternative** teaching and learning opportunities.

Bus-stop 2 Bus-stop™ Basics

The idea behind the Bus-stop 2 Bus-stop™ learning method is that students will be exposed to academic content starting at the school bus stop. Students will continue to be exposed to academic content throughout their school hours until they get dropped off at that same bus stop at the end of the school day. The name Bus-stop 2 Bus-stop™ was created because this method constantly exposes students, in many different and entertaining ways, to academic content from each "bus stop to bus stop." Since some students will not ride the school bus, this name is figurative in nature. Some students walk to school, skateboard, ride a bicycle, drive (or ride in) a car, etc.

Since some of the Bus-stop 2 Bus-stop™ learning areas are not supervised by an adult, the method serves as a means for nurturing independent learners. This method plays an important role not only in shaping the school's culture but also encouraging children to learn on their own. The corresponding research for this method is derived from brain-based learning, visual learning, **repetition** learning, social learning, incidental learning, and other teaching and learning aspects.

Development of the Idea

In the fall of 2010, Dr. Keshia L. Gaines began developing the Bus-stop 2 Bus-stop™ learning method. She formed the idea while trying to decorate her classroom with educational posters. After putting posters with academic content on the majority of her walls, she still had a lot of posters left. She looked over at her classroom's ugly winter-green garbage can. "Why can't the garbage can be a learning tool?" she asked herself. She took a poster with phonic sounds and vocabulary words and wrapped it around the garbage can. It was no longer just a garbage can. It was a learning opportunity and a new tool for students to be exposed to unexpected and additional academic content. Dr. Gaines could now use the garbage can in a game or as part of a quiz review. Why not? The students look at objects that are in the classroom. Every student who used the garbage can had to look at the exterior to see how to throw in the trash. In the following months, Dr. Gaines continued to write, research, and record this unique learning method.

Dr. Gaines's Beliefs

1. Clothing worn to school by students, teachers, staff, and administrators should serve some educational purpose.
2. Areas of the school, such as the school cafeteria, playgrounds, and bathrooms should serve an educational purpose.
3. T-shirts and other school related clothing made for school use and wear should include educational content.
4. Students should be learning educational content at the bus stop and on the school bus.
5. School superintendents, principals, and other staff members should **troubleshoot** methods to turn non-academic times during the school day into academic learning opportunities.
6. There should be very little, if any, time during the school day when students are not exposed to academic content.
7. All classified staff should serve some sort of educational purpose. Example: the janitors should wear uniforms with educational content and also have a janitor's cart with additional educational content on it.
8. All staff members should have an introductory amount of educational administration training.

This picture shows several educational products
such as posters, clothing, cafeteria placemats, and a basketball
designed by Dr. Gaines.

Lunch with Dr. Gaines:
An Informal Teacher Interview

Dr. Gaines: Alright, thank you Teacher A for allowing me to interview you about learning outside the classroom. My first question for you today is "What is your **perspective** on learning outside the classroom during the school day?"

Teacher A: Um, my perspective is that there are many missed learning opportunities during the day. Children come to school with preconceived notions of what learning is supposed to be, and teachers do as well. We need to look at all opportunities and ways that we can reach children on different levels.

Dr. Gaines: . . . and with you being a gifted teacher and all . . . I know you work hard with your gifted students. How much time would you be willing to put into learning about teaching outside the classroom?

Teacher A: Well, all teachers are required to participate in professional development and I am willing to participate in any workshop, quarter, or semester work. I think any teacher would be willing to participate too.

Dr. Gaines: Do you know of any missed learning opportunities that you can identify during your student's schedule? Not something that is just your fault, but a time when they are not receiving academic content.

Teacher A: Oh, yeah . . . . students just sit around and socialize in the cafeteria and at the end of the school day. You know, I participated in a gifted workshop where a director of gifted ed. in a school engaged children in learning in the cafeteria. It was a question and answer period of what every third grader should know. It was fun, like trivia questions. It was a fun time! Children would go home and try to research the subject. "Who's the sixteenth president of the United States?" "What are the oceans of the world?"

Dr. Gaines: . . . right, right, that's a good idea.

Dr. Gaines: In your opinion, how many minutes of a student's daily schedule are non-instructional?

Teacher A: Oooh, well I don't have a clear idea since I am specialized and I do a pull-out program, but I would assume, being from my former background as a regular classroom teacher . . . at least an hour to an hour and a half. I'm just making a good guess.

Dr. Gaines: Okay. Uum, what do you think about a program or workshop that is used to explain or utilize missed learning opportunities? . . . the non-instructional times in a student's day. Do you think a program, an instructional program, would be able to help?

Teacher A: . . . sure . . .

Dr. Gaines: Do you think it will be able to help the teachers?

Teacher A: I think it will help gain knowledge on how to make students learn better. I'm sure all teachers are open to that idea.

Dr. Gaines: Okay . . . uum . . . well having said that, could providing instructional review during this missed learning opportunity increase academic achievement?

Teacher A: Yes, I think so. I think if we expose students to a situation at least four times, it becomes a learning opportunity. Children learn by repetition.

Dr. Gaines: Okay . . . well, we said teachers, but what about the administrators and other staff members. How do you think they will view an opportunity to increase learning opportunities?

Teacher A: Well, I don't really know. I think every administration in every district has a different set of goals or **objectives** . . . but educators should use every opportunity they can to enhance student learning.

Dr. Gaines: okay . . . uum . . . well, how would the students view the loss of their down-times or **transition** times? In the hallways, cafeteria, other places where they are not receiving instruction. How do you think the students will react with those times being replaced by a learning opportunity?

Teacher A: I think it's all in the way that it is delivered. The delivery system is the key to the student "buying-in" to the idea if it is presented in a fun, interesting, very **innovative** way. They are learning something everyday, either positive or negative . . . so why not take this opportunity. I think they would be very receptive.

Dr. Gaines: Okay . . . uum . . . what about stakeholders? Do you think stakeholders would be willing to play the part in increasing instructional time?

Teacher A: Oh, I think that they could be a key component to working with children. Teachers and administrators are only going to be available to work with students at certain times. The other stakeholders could be on the school site when a teacher is not available. It would be great to have volunteers administer the system or to provide these opportunities.

Dr. Gaines: Okay . . . when we start talking about increasing student achievement, some people think about money. I mean, the budget is tight. The money is funny. Do you think that increasing these

	learning opportunities equates to more money being spent?
Teacher A:	. . . No . . .
Dr. Gaines:	What do you think about this issue?
Teacher A:	I think it has been proven in the past that you can throw money at education all day long, and it will not affect student achievement as much as committed educators and a delivery system that makes learning fun and makes it . . . uuh . . . hands-on. The child has to take ownership of their learning. They have to become a part of the system, not just a receiver of it. They have to have ownership in their own education. It's not about money. It's about innovation and making learning fun.
Dr. Gaines:	Okay (Pause)
Teacher A:	Oh, and to piggy back on that, children have TV's, video games, etc. nowadays. They are used to being entertained. They are so used to being a receiver. They need to be a part of the whole process. Their success is the success of their school.
Dr. Gaines:	. . . so . . . not just changing the amount of learning opportunities, but trying to change the culture of students so they will take responsibility for their own education?
Teacher A:	Exactly . . . exactly
Dr. Gaines:	. . . right . . . okay . . .
Teacher A:	. . . to light that fire and desire for them . . . to **acquire** knowledge and be personally responsible for their own achievement.

Dr. Gaines: Well . . . I know, Teacher A, we've had lunch a few times . . . and we have had time to troubleshoot and identify missed learning opportunities within the school.

Teacher A: . . . yeah . . .

Dr. Gaines: What do you think about learning outside the classroom as far as cognitive learning or brain-based learning? Could this be one of the main focuses or problems with education?

Teacher A: I think that's it for sure! I do. I totally agree with that. I think we have so many opportunities that children could be engaged in some type of learning activity, and they are not even aware of it.

Dr. Gaines: . . . right . . .

Teacher A: . . . and you see these kids . . . they know every word to every popular song on the radio. So why can't they know the continents or the multiplication facts?

Dr. Gaines: . . . right . . . you're right . . .

Teacher A: . . . and we are failing in math because they do not have the basic computation skills they need to know. They cannot retain them.

Dr. Gaines: . . . . yeah . . .

Teacher A: . . . and why can they not retain them?

Dr. Gaines: (silence)

Teacher A: They are not practiced at home. Our cultures are so diverse now. The parents may be separated or working. To make up for this, we could provide extra learning opportunities in out-of the-box areas like the school cafeteria.

Dr. Gaines: . . . right, right.

Teacher A: If they had some type of fun while they are eating, maybe a catchy tune, they would pick it up . . . they will pick it up. No one says they have to learn all the words to a song. They just pick it up.

Dr. Gaines: . . . right . . . right.

Teacher A: . . . yep . . .

Dr. Gaines: . . . and even the music business uses repetition. You turn on the radio and you say you don't like a song at first. But after they play it over and over again . . . in traffic, etc., you are getting that repetition—and that is the key.

Teacher A: . . . they do . . . they do . . .

Dr. Gaines: yeah . . . and I even noticed the playground. Kickball. They kick the ball, run around the bases and that's it. Could even things like that be a learning opportunity?

Teacher A: Oh, I think so . . . very much so. I think the P.E. area could present the game with learning in it. Geometry: "You are going in a triangle." That is an opportunity. They could learn vocabulary words in the P.E. department. You could have them posted . . . like you say . . .

Dr. Gaines: . . . . right, right . . .

Teacher A: . . . on the bases . . . First base is a square. "First" Second base. Those numbers and relationships. I see there are all types of opportunities. This could be for the younger children and then it could progress to high school level.

Dr. Gaines: Well, now since we mention P.E., you can do it with any other elective class like music, library, and other things.

Teacher A: . . . unh, hunh . . .

Dr. Gaines: I designed my educational clothing line so that teachers, students, and others can be exposed to visual learning opportunities.

Teacher A: . . . unh, hunh . . .

Dr. Gaines: I mean, the kids stare at teachers all day. They are getting that visual . . . that repetition. And if they stare at our clothes that says 2+2, maybe one day it will be 4!

Dr. Gaines: (laughing)

Teacher A: (laughing) . . . well, maybe . . .

Dr. Gaines: (laughing continued) Well, we hope so.

Teacher A: Like you say, every avenue, every time you are engaged, you are learning something.

Dr. Gaines: . . . you're right . . .

Teacher A: In our district, we have a time at the end of the day where students sit in line, kindergarten through sixth grade. They sit on the floor completely quiet. That 30 minutes could be the most fun learning time of their day. You have undivided attention there.

Dr. Gaines: . . . right . . . . right . . . .

Teacher A: It could be an interactive fun time, math facts, or maybe a story time.

Dr. Gaines: . . . oh, sure . . .

Teacher A: They couldn't wait to get back to answer the trivia question or hear the ending of a good children's story.

Dr. Gaines: . . . . oh, and I agree with you. For 30 minutes, I observe students waiting for their parents at the end of the school day. The children are just sitting there.

Teacher A: . . . . un . . . hunh . . . .

Dr. Gaines: I figure as long as children are on school property, a learning opportunity should be present. That's just my philosophy. I am eager to expose my learning techniques to schools in the United States.

Teacher A: Well, Dr. Gaines, I wish you much success in your plans for transforming American schools.

Discussion Questions for Chapter 1

1. In your opinion, what are two things that should be changed about America's education system? Why?
2. How could America's public and private schools benefit from the Bus-stop 2 Bus-stop™ learning method?
3. In your opinion, do American students waste too much time during the school day? Why or why not?
4. What are the five main areas for learning with the Bus-stop 2 Bus-stop™ method?
5. In the informal interview with Dr. Gaines, what were Teacher A's feelings towards new learning methods?

Journal Activity for Chapter 1

Write a song or poem about the Bus-stop 2 Bus-stop™ learning method using the information you learned in chapter one. Pretend that you are creating a radio commercial script or jingle to advertise the Bus-stop 2 Bus-stop™ method on the radio.

Vocabulary Word Review for Chapter 1

The following words were discussed in Chapter 1. On a separate sheet of paper, complete the following four steps for each word shown below.

- ✓ Write the word's definition (from a dictionary).
- ✓ Draw a picture to help you remember the word's meaning.
- ✓ Create a 2-3 word definition of the word.
- ✓ Write one or more sentences using the word.

repetition	transition
perspective	alternative
troubleshoot	implemented
acquire	significant
innovative	objectives

Fun Activity for Chapter 1

Draw a picture of a classroom garbage can with academic content on the exterior. Write an explanation about how the garbage can could be used in a game or classroom lesson.

Chapter 2

The Bus Stop: The First Area for Learning

Why are students not learning at the bus stop?

The first area for academic **exposure** with the Bus-stop 2 Bus-stop™ learning method is the bus stop. **Traditionally**, students in America stand at the bus stop for a varied amount of time (**approximately** 10-15 minutes) waiting for the school bus. This time can be turned into a learning opportunity if the bus stop bench and surrounding areas included **academic**

content similar to the **advertisements** that businesses use to sell their services and products. Schools can also use ground signage and folders allocated for students to study at the bus stop. Since students can learn **independently** at the bus stop, teachers could provide an **incentive** or reward for students who bring their folders on a daily basis. Similarly, walking and car riding students can **benefit** from the study folder also. Since all students do not ride the school bus, some student's first Bus-stop 2 Bus-stop™ experience may be the school's sidewalks or hallways.

The Classroom is Too Late

Dr. Gaines believes that the classroom should not be the first area to expose students to learning. "The classroom is too late," Gaines explains. "Students have already spent up to one hour of non-instructional time." This includes standing at the bus stop, eating breakfast in the cafeteria, and unstructured socializing with peers. Gaines points out that the morning is the best time for students to learn because they are well rested and alert. "If students started getting exposure to academic content at the bus stop, this would greatly reduce educational down time," Gaines adds.

Another one of the main focuses with the Bus-stop 2 Bus-stop™ method is increasing the actual learning time of students. When students stand at the bus stop, they can be exposed to academic content while waiting for the bus. Since academic "down time" is a big concern, this chapter focuses on how increasing academic learning time will increase academic **achievement**.

17

How could learning at the bus stop help academic achievement?

Many aspects of education have changed over the years, therefore, schools should accommodate these changes. Even though the curriculum changes often, there have been very minimal changes in terms of time **allocated** for learning curriculum. There are also many advancements of technology in the education system which creates more demands for educators, in terms of time. Increasing learning time means adding to the length of a school day, week, or year. The objective of additional time is restructuring the school for greater focus on academic achievement. Programs and activities that increase learning time are very effective because they give students more opportunities to learn. This topic has prompted a lot of research to investigate the effect of increasing academic learning time. Parts of the school day used for learning academic content are seen as something that educators and school administrators can control. Some of these are ensuring time-on-task, effective transitioning periods, and fewer disruptions in the classroom. One method to increase learning time is for students to learn academic content at the bus stop.

Academic Learning Time and Student Success

There is a positive relationship between learning time and student success. In other words, the more time spent on learning, the more successful students can become. However, this relationship is quite complicated. This is because simply increasing learning time will not automatically result in increased academic achievement. Unfortunately, not all academic time for instruction is actually spent on instruction. For example, a one hour class may include several minutes of distributing worksheets and several minutes of student interruptions leaving only a small amount of time for instruction.

Learning Variations Across Classrooms and Schools

Studies have recorded significant time variations across classrooms and schools. Despite the differences, teachers often allocate homework for additional learning time. For example, one teacher may allocate 30 minutes worth of homework, while another teacher allocates only 10 minutes worth. Variations in homework assignments and class structures means that the total allocated time for students will vary greatly. The differences between the allocated time and the time required for learning varies with students inside the classroom. Some believe that educators need to analyze learning differences in order to determine the amount of time required for each student to master the content. Instructional time refers to the proportion of time that is actually used for instructional activities. There are various activities that take place in classrooms that may affect the amount of time that is allocated for instructional purposes. To get a true estimate of instructional time, a researcher must deduct activities and other distractions. The amount of time that is spent on other activities besides instructional ones is referred to as "down time" or "lost time."

Let's Make up for Summer Vacation

Summer vacation is a common term in the United States educational system. It is a vacation during the summer period between school years, when most schools are not in session. During this time, the students and teachers are out of school from six to 12 weeks. This period varies widely within states and districts. There has been much support as well as criticism for this holiday. Supporters of summer vacation state that the few weeks offered by the vacation are to relax. Others believe that the summer vacation should be eliminated. Many opponents of summer vacation have argued that schools in the United States spend fewer days in school per school year, when compared to schools in other countries. Several researchers in the United States stated that having such a long vacation puts American students at a disadvantage.

There have been requests to reshape the structure of the school day and school year to increase learning time and academic performance. Various professionals have pointed out the major flaws of America's public education system such as the dropout rate and student illiteracy percentages. Increasing learning time means having a longer school day, week, or year to significantly increase the total number of school hours for learning. Some view additional learning time to be a solution to increasing academic achievement. This is supported by the argument that the current structure of the school day and year is not conducive to improving academic achievement. Sometimes, when children are out of school for summer vacation, parents feel obligated to give their children learning activities so they will not regress. Some parents even enroll their children in private summer schools. Another way to increase learning time is to allow students to learn at nontraditional areas such as the school bus stop.

Learning at the Bus Stop

A school day consists of the beginning of school (when students arrive at school) until school ends (when students leave school). In other words, a school day is "from bus-stop to bus-stop." As a secondary student, you can take advantage of time spent standing at the bus stop.

Learning is not confined to classrooms. This means that students do not only learn when they are seated in the classroom and there is a teacher instructing them. Many times, the best opportunities for learning occur outside the classroom. Just as adults continue to learn more every day of their lives, children are learning constantly as well. The primary focus should be learning academic content instead of non-academic material. Whether before school, during meals in school, after school, or even during the weekend, there are great avenues to encourage innovative ways of learning outside the classroom. Often times, lunch or recess is a student's favorite part of the school day. A very small percentage of students will admit to enjoying instruction time in the classroom. As a result, the educational system should be structured in such a way that every experience during the school day is an opportunity for learning.

The learning process can take place both with student awareness and without student awareness. Researchers call this "incidental learning" or "non-conscious learning." Without student awareness, non-conscious learning can happen as a student is playing outside and recognizes something that the teacher has taught in the classroom. It may happen when a student encounters something during lunch or recess and remembers it in class when the teacher introduces the topic. Learning outside the classroom, in areas like the school bus stop, creates an engaging environment that encourages children to reach their full potential. These avenues for learning are especially effective due to the fact that students learn more as they do things they enjoy. Additionally, when students learn through real life experiences, they are in a much better position to remember the academic content. There are many different ways that may help improve our current education system. The most important concept is transforming students' non-educational time into academic opportunities.

Discussion Questions for Chapter 2

1. What are some ways that schools could integrate technology with learning at the bus stop?
2. What is incidental learning? How can it be implemented at a school bus stop?
3. According to this chapter, what is one advantage and one disadvantage of students having a summer vacation?
4. Why does Dr. Gaines believe students should be exposed to academic content at the school bus stop?
5. In your opinion, what age group of students would be most successful while learning at the bus stop? (Elementary, Middle School, or High School) Why?

Journal Activity for Chapter 2

Draw a picture of five students standing at a school bus stop. Include a bus stop bench and some in-ground signs that include academic content. Write 5 or more sentences that describe your scene.

Vocabulary Word Review for Chapter 2

The following words were discussed in Chapter 2. On a separate sheet of paper, complete the following four steps for each word shown below.

- ✓ Write the word's definition (from a dictionary).
- ✓ Draw a picture to help you remember the word's meaning.
- ✓ Create a 2-3 word definition of the word.
- ✓ Write one or more sentences using the word.

benefit	approximately
exposure	incentive
achievement	allocated
traditionally	independently
academic	advertisements

Fun Activity for Chapter 2

Draw a picture and create a simple model of a school bus stop with academic content. Write an explanation about how the bus stop area could use technology to teach students an educational game or classroom lesson at the school bus stop.

CHAPTER 3

The School Bus: A Yellow Classroom

Why are students not learning on the school bus?

For many years, students have been **transported** to and from school by school buses. School districts spend millions of dollars nationally to provide a variety of transportation for students. However, these funds spent on student transportation could also provide an educational benefit if students were exposed to academic content while on the buses.

The interior and exterior of a traditional school bus in America is basically the same in all parts of the country. Most school busses have a bright yellow exterior and a uniform interior, which usually includes the bus driver's area and large bus seats for the students. The large backs of the bus seats are a perfect opportunity to provide educational content. Also, television screens could be mounted on school buses, if funds were available. Learning programs should play while a student is riding to and from school. This would greatly increase academic exposure. The academic content should reflect the types of students on that bus route. For example, a bus route with high school students should **display** high school content on the television screens, while middle or elementary school bus routes should display materials tailored to their specific learning levels.

An **inexpensive** way to use this method is to attach small posters or cards, with academic content, above each window on the interior of the bus. This could serve an academic purpose and remind students of their assigned seats. Another inexpensive way to add academic opportunities on the school bus is to add an audio system, which can play catchy songs with academic content. This **auditory** learning method is better than not providing a learning opportunity at all, but it will have a lesser impact than a visual learning system or a visual learning system with audio.

In considering the larger **context** of academic content, school buses should include academic content on the exterior of the bus, just as city buses advertise on their exteriors. Specific bus routes could have assigned bus seats with specific study content and study partners. The school could hire a traveling bus tutor to assist students while learning on the school bus. The school bus has been an area of missed learning opportunity for years!

New Invention by Dr. Gaines:
The Universal School Bus Seat Learning Pad

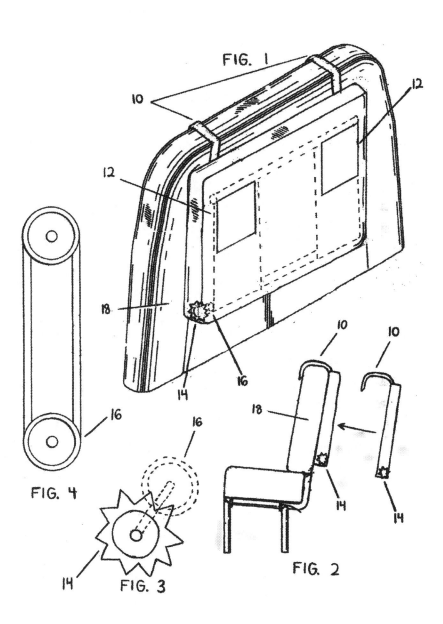

Overview of Invention

Purpose of Invention

The purpose of this **invention** is to provide a learning opportunity for children riding the school bus. Ultimately, this learning opportunity will increase overall academic achievement because children can learn from non-traditional areas. This invention gives students an additional opportunity to learn during the school day.

Brief Description of Invention

This invention is a learning system which is mounted on the back of a school bus seat for educational purposes. In addition, the invention includes **transparent** windows for viewing the academic content within. The front surface allows the inserting of various posters which display academic content. The interior of the learning system consists of a **pulley** with academic content on the pulley belt. The posters and academic content on the pulley belts can be interchanged as needed to meet the academic levels of the children on a **specific** bus route. Another version of this invention includes an electronic pad with touch screen electronic games and learning activities.

Description of the Problems Solved by the Invention

This invention will increase the academic achievement of students on the school bus. Since many students in America are not meeting their academic expectations (and potential)

in the general classroom, it is important to consider all methods and areas for students to learn. The school bus will be an additional area for learning that will help students increase academic achievement. Also, The Universal School Bus Seat Learning Pad will provide something positive (and educational) for students to do while riding the school bus.

How the Invention is an Improvement Over Existing Technology

This invention is the first known learning system designed especially for the back of a school bus seat. Other electronic and non-electronic products are designed for classroom and in-school use only. Many learning systems require electricity or battery use, but this invention works without additional energy sources. Students simply turn the knob on the learning pad to view the academic content on the pulley belt.

Groups of People that Would Use the Invention

The target groups may include all school districts (public schools and private schools), daycares, summer camp programs, church groups, non-profit organizations, and others that transport children or young adults by a school bus.

Benefits to Users of the Invention

This invention will provide many opportunities for students to learn while riding the school bus. It will also help users learn important educational content and improve on their report cards, classroom performance, and quizzes/ tests. The Universal School Bus Seat Learning Pad will provide something positive and educational for students to entertain themselves with while riding the school bus.

Descriptions of the Illustrations

Figure 1 is an enlarged side angle view of the Universal School Bus Seat Learning Pad attached to the back of a typical school bus seat.

Figure 2 shows the left side view of the invention attached to the back of a typical school bus seat. Also, Figure 2 shows a left side view of the invention by itself.

Figure 3 shows the turning **mechanism** of the pulley belt in greater detail.

Figure 4 is a side view of a pulley belt used in the invention. Many different types of academic content can be attached to the pulley belt. The academic content can be easily interchanged.

Reference numeral and Descriptive name for part

10—Curved attachment hooks

12—Transparent viewing windows

14—Turning knob for pulley belt

16—Pulley belt wheel with a grooved rim

18—Back rest of a school bus seat (not part of this invention—for visual demonstration only)

The invention operates by students turning a knob which then turns a pulley belt which displays academic content. The passenger may view the content on the enclosed pulley belt through the transparent windows. Since this version of the invention is manually operated, the passenger may turn the knob at his or her desired pace.

Unique Features of the Invention

1. Interchangeable pulley belt with academic content
2. Manually operated
3. Universal for mounting on the back of any size school bus seat

Alternative Versions of this Invention

1. Solar powered pulley belts which includes a solar panel on the top of the school bus
2. Battery powered pulley belts
3. Various sizes, shapes, and materials to make invention
4. Hooks that allow the invention to be screwed or bolted to the bus seat
5. An electronic pad version with touch screen electronic games and learning activities.

Discussion Questions for Chapter 3

1. What is the importance of a peer helper on a school bus?
2. In what ways can students benefit from a traveling school bus tutor on the school bus?
3. In your opinion, can The Universal School Bus Seat Learning Pad be altered and used in other areas of the school? Why or why not?

4. What are two items that can help children learn while on the school bus?
5. How is learning in the classroom similar to learning on the school bus?

Journal Activity for Chapter 3

Plan and sketch a school bus seating chart that encourages social learning. Imagine the bus has 20 3rd grade students (on grade level) and 20 6th grade students (on grade level). Write 5-6 sentences about your seating chart and explain any assigned bus seats.

Vocabulary Word Review for Chapter 3

The following words were discussed in Chapter 3. On a separate sheet of paper, complete the following four steps for each word shown below.

✓ Write the word's definition (from a dictionary).
✓ Draw a picture to help you remember the word's meaning.
✓ Create a 2-3 word definition of the word.
✓ Write one or more sentences using the word.

context	transparent
invention	specific
transported	pulley
display	inexpensive
mechanism	auditory

Fun Activity for Chapter 3

Interview two people about learning outside the classroom. Use the interview in Chapter 1 as a guide. Write a short summary of your interviews.

Scan the QR Code below to watch a video about "learning on the school bus."

CHAPTER 4

The Cafeteria: Academics for Breakfast and Lunch

Why are students not learning in the school cafeteria?

The school cafeteria is yet another overlooked area for learning. Dr. Gaines points out the importance of including academic content in the cafeteria. On average, students spend 10-15 minutes in the cafeteria for breakfast and 20-30 minutes in the cafeteria for lunch. This breakfast and lunch time can be multiplied by five school days a week. In most cases, students visit the school cafeteria at least once daily for lunch, whether he or she brings lunch or eats a school lunch. Since most school cafeterias allow student **socialization**, the cafeteria becomes useful as a social learning area.

In most elementary and middle schools in America, students are supervised in the cafeteria by their teachers. While students are eating, they can be exposed to academic content on educational placemats, television screens, posters, and other **visual** aids. Recent research shows that **alternative** learning areas (such as the school cafeteria) have **explicit** and direct connections to learning. Learning in the school cafeteria with television screens, educational placemats, small posters, etc. is a safe way to educate students without requiring major changes.

The Breakfast Club: A Healthy Way to Learn

An example of a research study where students had increased learning time in the cafeteria was called the Breakfast Club. This study mixed breakfast time with structured and interesting learning activities. In this study, in order to accommodate the breakfast club, the school day needed to be extended to begin earlier than the normal time. The Breakfast Club was an effective avenue for promotion of nutrition and academic content during a usually informal and overlooked learning opportunity. The club provided at least one additional learning task to each breakfast. In addition, the Breakfast Club was a healthy way to start the school day, which is crucial for learning.

A Cafeteria Placemat Research Study by Dr. Gaines

For her dissertation, Dr. Keshia L. Gaines conducted a research study using various educational placemats in a school cafeteria. Her dissertation title is *A Quantitative Study of Learning in the School Cafeteria Using Educational Placemats*. In this research study, Dr. Gaines studied the differences in student achievement before and after students were **exposed** to educational placemats in a school cafeteria for four days each with four different placemats. The student's gender and ability grouping was considered in relation to achievement. This study included 49 ability grouped third grade students in an elementary school in south Mississippi. Students were pre-tested with researcher-made tests before the educational placemats were introduced and post-tested afterwards. See the descriptive information about the pre-tests, post-tests, and placemats in the table below.

PRE-TESTS, POST-TESTS, AND PLACEMATS

Order	Color	Content	Corresponding Test
Placemat #1	Yellow	Fractions	Fractions Tests
Placemat #2	Pink	Solar System	Lines/Angles Test
Placemat #3	Teal	2D and 3D Shapes	Shapes Test
Placemat #4	Light Blue	Parts of Speech	Perimeter Test

For research purposes, some of the placemats served as a control factor and did not relate to the pre-test and post-test content. Dr. Gaines measured the differences in scores using statistical software. Two of the **hypotheses** proposed a significant increase in learning (pre-test and post-test) by both gender and ability group. After being exposed to math placemats, the post-test scores were significantly higher than the pre-test scores across both genders and groups. In contrast, after exposure to the control placemats, post-test scores across genders and groups were lower than pre-test scores and did not significantly differ.

The cafeteria placemats with math (same concepts on cafeteria placemats and tests) showed a significant academic improvement after cafeteria placemat exposure. In other words, students had higher testing averages after exposure to math educational placemats in the school cafeteria. In contrast, the cafeteria placemats without math showed a decrease in test averages after cafeteria placemat exposure. There were higher scores on the post-tests after exposure to placemats with mathematical content.

Music and Audio in the School Cafeteria

Many **formal** and fast food restaurants use music and audio advertising to **persuade** customers. In this same fashion, schools can use music or audio in the school cafeteria to change the student's moods and teach academic content. It is very important that the school cafeteria creates a welcoming atmosphere for relaxation and social learning.

Tools to Implement Learning in the Cafeteria

1. Use educational placemats on the cafeteria tables
2. Use TV screens with educational programming
3. Use audio (music) to **alter** mood, behavior, or to educate
4. Use small posters on the cafeteria tables
5. Use educational content on the **interior** walls of the cafeteria

Discussion Questions for Chapter 4

1. What are three tools that can help students learn academic content in the school cafeteria?

2. In your opinion, do you think teacher supervision will affect the successfulness of learning in the school cafeteria?

3. How does "The Breakfast Club" help students learn in the school cafeteria?

4. How is learning in the school cafeteria similar to learning on the school bus?

5. According to this workbook, what is the average time spent in the school cafeteria for breakfast and lunch? In your opinion, what subject area should students learn during this time?

Journal Activity for Chapter 4

Observe one formal restaurant and one fast food restaurant. Write 5 ways that school cafeterias are alike and different from public restaurants.

Vocabulary Word Review for Chapter 4

The following words were discussed in Chapter 4. On a separate sheet of paper, complete the following four steps for each word shown below.

✓ Write the word's definition (from a dictionary).
✓ Draw a picture to help you remember the word's meaning.
✓ Create a 2-3 word definition of the word.
✓ Write one or more sentences using the word.

hypotheses	explicit
interior	alternative
formal	visual
persuade	alter
socialization	exposed

Fun Activity for Chapter 4

Draw a cafeteria placemat for teaching elementary or high school students. Include at least two subject areas, five vocabulary words, and one cartoon character.

CHAPTER 5

The Bathroom: An Independent Study and Other Controversial Areas to Learn

Why are students not learning in other non-traditional areas?

Traditionally, students have used the school's bathroom for more than toiletry needs. Fights, bullying, cursing, and even drug use occurs in many school bathrooms of the twenty-first century. Negative actions of all sorts have reportedly taken place in elementary, middle, and high school bathroom stalls across America. Students realize that the inside of the bathroom has very little, if any, supervision by teachers and staff. School leaders and others can prevent a school's bathroom area from becoming a **haven** for bullying, skipping class, or drug and tobacco use. Scan the QR code below to read an article about how to stop school bullying.

Unlike other Bus-stop 2 Bus-stop™ methods, a school's bathroom can serve as a brief and independent study session. Instead of using school bathrooms for toiletry needs only, an educational component should be present. This educational component can take form as academic posters, television screens, and/or audio systems. Adding educational components to the interior of a school's bathroom could serve two purposes:

1. Purpose #1—Adding educational content to the school's bathroom will increase academic achievement. Research has shown, in current literature, how incidental learning benefits students.
2. Purpose #2—Adding educational content to the school's bathroom may decrease the amount of fights, bullying, cursing, and even drug use. Research has

shown that students are less likely to get into trouble if they are in a structured environment with purpose.

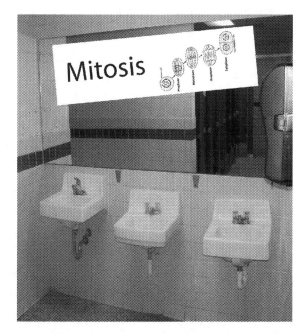

School bathrooms consist of separate areas for boys and girls. With this in mind, a school administrator can plan gender-specific academic designs for each bathroom's interior. Learning styles and preferences differ amongst boys and girls. In some cases, mathematic achievement is related to a student's gender and interest in mathematics. Using current data, a school can pinpoint their academic areas of concern according to a gender breakdown.

Gender roles are very important in today's society. When children are young, parents buy toys, clothes, and other items according to a child's gender. **Stereotypical** careers are mentioned for boys such as a doctor, lawyer, engineer, or even President of the United States. In contrast, parents may mention careers for girls, but many parents still assume that one day their daughters will grow into the role of a wife and mother. Society has certain **expectations** for boys that differ from the expectations for girls. These expectations generate varying patterns of behavior and reactions according to the child's gender. Gender roles should be considered when designing a gender-specific bathroom area for students.

The choir room, football stadium, gym, tennis court, and swimming pool areas can use the Bus-stop 2 Bus-stop™ method to increase student exposure to academic content. In consideration of the school's goal for academic achievement outside the classroom, extra-curricular activities should use the Bus-stop 2 Bus-stop™ method as well. The classroom is an **obvious** place that academic content should be displayed. Before using the Bus-stop 2 Bus-stop™ method, a school's administration and staff should examine the school and community's culture. Schools that embrace student learning are more likely to be successful with the Bus-stop 2 Bus-stop™ learning method.

In order to **enhance** student learning, schools must encourage students to learn in areas outside the classroom. Educational activities in non-traditional areas, such as the school gym, choir room, and video arcade rooms, will provide a valued learning experience for the student. According to past research, out-of-classroom exposure to educational material is beneficial because it exposes students to the following things:

1. Complex thinking skills
2. Social skills with peers
3. Application of knowledge

4. Building self-confidence and individuality
5. Decision making
6. Social learning opportunities

How can schools implement this?

First and foremost, schools should **analyze** their school environment. Starting at the bus stop, school stakeholders should examine all school areas to find new areas for teaching and learning. After these non-traditional areas are identified, a plan should be put into place to change these areas into learning opportunities.

The Educational Video Arcade

A video arcade room can be a fun alternative learning area. In addition to the educational component, some games can mix exercise with educational content and engaging games. Usually, video arcade games are in public businesses such as movie theatres, restaurants, amusement parks, local fairs, etc. Most games are categorized as pinball games, electronic video games, games to win **merchandise**, or sports and recreation games.

Coin-operated machines provide a fun, engaging atmosphere for youth and teens. The 1920's amusement park inspired today's arcade games. As early as the 1930's, coin-operated pinball machines were used. Why can't schools offer educational games as an alternative learning opportunity or as an incentive for good behavior?

Children enjoy games that involve scoring points, animations, racing games, vehicle combat games (most are equipped with joysticks and buttons), and **repetitive** memory games.

Music Recording Studio

Some students enjoy writing and recording music. Since music and rhythm helps students learn academic content, students should have an area to create and record music on the school campus. The music teacher can create lessons that **integrate** math, language, and other curriculums with music. The recording sessions may be awarded as an incentive or as a part of a **mandatory** class assignment.

Automated Teacher Robots

As an alternative, some students could rely on automated teachers to ask and answer questions about academic content. These automated teacher robots can assist students during educational down times and transitions. Giving students a choice is one of the most important lesson design qualities. Some students may prefer to work individually with computerized lessons from an automated teacher robot. This unique learning robot for the future will provide students with an alternative method for learning.

Amusement Park Type School:
The Schools of the Future

Imagine a non-stop fun learning experience in your school. Color, music, and hands on activities could be mixed with academic content. At a glance, the school would look similar to a local carnival or fun park. At second glance, a bystander would realize that all games, activities, etc. are related to district, state, and national academic standards. Any classroom instruction would take place solely to help students with writing, formal lessons, and test taking.

Discussion Questions for Chapter 5

1. In your opinion, what is the best method for students to learn academic content in the school bathroom? Video, audio, or posters as visual aids?
2. How is learning in the bathroom alike and different from learning in the school cafeteria?
3. In your opinion, which age group and gender will receive the greatest benefit from learning in the bathroom? Boys or girls? High school, middle school, or elementary students?
4. What two purposes could be served by adding an educational video arcade room to an elementary school?
5. What makes (or does not make) the school bathroom a controversial area for students to learn? Why?

Journal Activity for Chapter 5

Using a computer program, design one boy's bathroom and one girl's bathroom with math and language themed content. Use gender-specific colors, themes, and items for student interest. Write five or more sentences that explain your designs.

Vocabulary Word Review for Chapter 5

The following words were discussed in Chapter 5. On a separate sheet of paper, complete the following four steps for each word shown below.

- ✓ Write the word's definition (from a dictionary).
- ✓ Draw a picture to help you remember the word's meaning.
- ✓ Create a 2-3 word definition of the word.
- ✓ Write one or more sentences using the word.

obvious	merchandise
expectations	analyze
stereotypical	enhance
integrate	haven
mandatory	repetitive

Fun Activity for Chapter 5

Write a short summary and draw a picture of how you would add a learning opportunity to the interior of the following school areas: choir room, football stadium, and gym.

CHAPTER 6

The Playground: A Fun Place to Learn

Why are students not learning on the playground?

The playground should be **targeted** as a primary area for students to learn academic content. Since most students enjoy visiting and playing on the playground, their interest level is very high. The playground can become an area for brain-based learning because it mixes physical movement, academic content, and high student interest. This mixture relates to brain-based learning and brain-based education, which are methods the brain learns best.

Learning on the Playground: An Early Window of Learning Opportunity

A person's window of learning opportunity will not occur again once it has passed. This window occurs in a person's early years of life. Educational salespersons take advantage of this knowledge and use it in various advertisements. There are numerous educational product companies that promote the links between their products and specific areas of brain development. Parents are urged to buy many products to **stimulate** development during their child's early years. Early learning tools and opportunities are very beneficial to youth and adolescents.

Every student has a different learning style. School teachers and other education **practitioners** support the idea of getting to know a student's learning style before beginning instruction. After the learning style has been identified, the educator can then apply the appropriate teaching techniques and methods to help the student. Many students respond to a lesson when it is taught using the learning style that the student prefers.

This is a picture of an educational basketball
designed by Dr. Gaines.

Educational Games on the Playground

Many teachers have shared the benefits of engaging
students by using social activities such as games. According
to these teachers, others should be mindful of how to make
learning engaging for students. Expert teachers agree that
games are a great way for students to learn, especially if the
student is a part of the design or **construction** of the game.
In the opinion of researchers, activities help young learners,
because they include movement. Movement and physical
exercise have been known to stimulate the students' brains.

Also, laughter inside and outside of the classroom is a brain-based approach. Researchers claim that the body **biochemically** reacts to humor. Also, humor helps to reduce stress and create a better **environment**. In addition to humor, it is a good idea to include activities with **manipulatives** and other visual aids. The following "musical school bus" game mixes a fun and engaging game with learning content.

"Musical School Bus" Game

Materials needed:

1. Several school bus shaped cutouts with test formatted questions on them (number the cards from 1-10 or more)
2. Answer sheet for the test-formatted questions
3. One music player

Directions: Gather 5-10 or more friends to play the Musical School Bus Game. Have each player hold one numbered school bus shaped cutout. Stand in a circle facing inward. Select an additional player to be in charge of the music. When the music starts, the players pass around their cutouts in a clockwise manner. When the music stops, players stop passing around the cutouts. The player with the lowest numbered cutout will attempt to answer the test-formatted question. If the player gets the answer wrong, he or she loses and leaves the circle. If the player gets the answer right, he or she gets to stay in the circle. Repeat this process. The last player standing wins!

Sidewalks Near the Playground and School: Walk and Learn

As students are walking from class to the playground, they **observe** the surroundings in the hallways. Many schools post student work samples, art projects, or other student work in the hallway, but do not include academic learning content. If academic content was added to the school's sidewalks, hallways, and floors, it would increase academic achievement of students.

A sidewalk usually connects the students getting off the school bus or out of their parent's vehicle to the school. Also, sidewalks often surround playgrounds, basketball courts, and other outside areas. Repetition, visual learning, and unintentional learning are evident when students are exposed to academic content in these playground areas.

Incidental Learning on the Playground

Incidental learning refers to the unintentional learning that results from informal activities. As a thought process, incidental learning takes place through repetition, observation, social interaction activities, and problem solving situations. Incidental learning may occur when a student unknowingly glances at the sidewalk or playground equipment while playing on the playground. Educators are able to analyze how learning from visual aids on physical education equipment or on a sidewalk can affect students.

Memory recall of random information among elementary students is usually greater with the usage of pictures than words. This is important to remember when creating learning opportunities for areas where students walk and play. In order to understand how incidental learning affects elementary students, it is important to note that this type of learning is unplanned. In most cases of incidental learning, a person will go through a learning experience without any previous intention of gaining something out of the experience. Even though it is unintentional, incidental learning affects the unconscious learning of a person by visual and auditory memory.

Another area where incidental learning affects the students at the elementary level is language or vocabulary learning development. This is because through observation and social interaction the students develop a visual association with the carefully designed hallways, sidewalks, and floors. At one point, they are able to associate the pictures and words written on the sidewalks with their existing knowledge on the subject. Furthermore, considering that incidental learning may occur outside the classroom in any Bus-stop 2 Bus-stop™ area, it may also tie into social learning. Playgrounds provide helpful learning environments because they are places where social interactions can take place.

A series of studies have confirmed that incidental learning can help children in multiple positive ways. Some of the effective ways in which incidental learning can help students is through improving their basic memory, especially in vocabulary, pictures, and mathematical concepts.

Another benefit of informal and incidental learning is the growth of social skills. Incidental learning in the form of observing a visual aid placed on the playground will most likely change the student's behavior and social interaction with other students. Some experts acknowledge that incidental learning occurs outside the traditional education context and provides a motivational and enjoyable opportunity for students to learn academic content. Incidental learning can also help in the **intellectual** development of an elementary and secondary student. It is noted that much of this learning happens easily, randomly, and beyond standard teaching in the classroom.

Discussion Questions for Chapter 6

1. How does movement and physical exercise help students learn academic content?
2. In your opinion, what subject areas would students learn best while on the playground?
3. How could schools ensure that students are exposed to academic content on the playground? (permanent displays, mandatory games, etc.)
4. What is incidental learning?
5. How is learning on the playground alike and different from the other Bus-stop 2 Bus-stop™ learning areas?

Journal Activity for Chapter 6

With the help of your teacher, write a simple lesson plan that is taught primarily on a school playground. Include hands on activities, writing assignments, etc. for students to complete on the school's playground. Include educational games for students to play on a nearby sidewalk. Include the use of sidewalk chalk.

Vocabulary Word Review for Chapter 6

The following words were discussed in Chapter 6. On a separate sheet of paper, complete the following four steps for each word shown below.

- ✓ Write the word's definition (from a dictionary).
- ✓ Draw a picture to help you remember the word's meaning.
- ✓ Create a 2-3 word definition of the word.
- ✓ Write one or more sentences using the word.

stimulate	environment
practitioners	manipulatives
construction	observe
targeted	incidental
biochemically	intellectual

Fun Activity for Chapter 6

Create your own educational game to learn math content on the playground. Write the rules and directions for the game. Include the number of players and materials needed.

CHAPTER 7

Bus-stop 2 Bus-stop™ Educational Clothing for Faculty, Staff, and Students

Why are students not learning from educational clothing?

BREAKING NEWS
Dr. Keshia L. Gaines "Makes Learning Stylish" with New Clothing Line Concept

Dr. Keshia L. Gaines has recently released her new "Bus-stop 2 Bus-stop™" Clothing Line. This new clothing line attracts youth, teens, and others by its unique method of including academic content and designs. This clothing line concept comes from chapter 7 of Dr. Gaines's ground-breaking book about learning outside the classroom.

Young doctor and entrepreneur Keshia L. Gaines, Ph.D. has partnered with international clothing manufacturer, Zazzle Apparel, to announce the launch of Bus-stop 2 Bus-stop™ Clothing (busstop2busstop.com). This new clothing line is a unique sportswear and casual collection based off of Gaines's active lifestyle and educational **philosophy**. "I'm launching this clothing line because it is educational, positive, and fun. My Bus-stop 2 Bus-stop™ Clothing Line 'makes learning stylish' for youth, teens, and others," stated Dr. Gaines.

Dr. Gaines's active lifestyle as an author and educator led her to create this ground-breaking clothing line. In her new book *"Why are Students Not Learning on the School Bus?"*(www.amazon.com), Dr. Gaines explains her philosophy towards education and unique learning methods. She believes that students should learn academic content outside the classroom by learning on the school bus, in the cafeteria, on the playground, in the bathrooms, from academic clothing, etc.

Inspired by Dr. Gaines's signature style, the clothing line features shirts, hats, tote bags, necklaces, jackets, and more with academic content and designs on them. Most of the designs feature the 1-12 multiplication facts and have a positive social meaning behind the particular math fact. According to Dr. Gaines, customers can buy Bus-stop 2 Bus-stop™ Clothing that supports volunteering, good character, education, the environment, and much more. "I like working on the details, designs, and marketing," said Dr. Gaines. "I am so excited about releasing the 1-12 multiplication fact chart with social meanings. Bus-stop 2 Bus-stop™ Clothing has had a really good response from youth and teens," she said.

Academic Clothing and Accessories: Learning in Style

According to Dr. Gaines's belief number one, "Clothing worn to school by students, teachers, staff, and administrators should serve some educational purpose." In alignment with this belief, Dr. Gaines has created a clothing line that expands across many subject areas and grade levels. The first Bus-stop 2 Bus-stop™ clothing items were made by Dr. Gaines to wear and display at her **dissertation** defense. They included two women's suit coat jackets with multiplication facts **embroidered** on them. Dr. Gaines wore a yellow suit coat jacket with 6 x 7 = 42 embroidered on the back. Her additional suit coat jacket was pink with 8 x 4= 32 embroidered on the back. As part of her dissertation defense, she illustrated the purposes of clothing in various professions.

Purposes of Clothing in Various Professions

Medical Doctor	Firefighter	Military Soldier	School Teacher
Surgical mask-conceals bacteria	Protective goggles-protects eyes	Steel-toed Boots-protects feet	Casual Shirts? ?
White lab coat-Protects clothes and skin	Fire-proof suit-Protects skin	Camouflage clothing-Disguises soldier	Casual Dress/Pants? ?

Medical doctors, firefighters, and military personnel wear clothing that reflect their overall career goal. The Bus-stop 2 Bus-stop™ method includes re-designing school staff and student clothing to reflect the school's overall goal, which is to increase student achievement. Students, teachers, and staff should wear clothing with academic content on the exterior of the clothing. Also, student uniforms should have multiplication facts, polygons, types of lines and angles, and other academic content to be learned by visual learning, social learning, and repetition.

Bus-stop 2 Bus-stop Clothing
"Makes Learning Stylish"

Dr. Gaines- Signature Collection

School Uniforms: A Touchy Subject

There are mixed feelings about the wearing of school uniforms. Uniforms are intended to create a **standardized** dress and **appearance** of togetherness and/or equality. Also, uniforms create a less judgmental **atmosphere** since all students wear similar or identical clothing regardless of race, class, or gender. However, some students, parents, and others dislike the use of school uniforms because it takes away the student's individual expression. Others argue that uniforms falsely represent the **diversity** of real-life society.

In contrast, uniforms such as sports uniforms provide a specific function. Colors and patterns of teams provide a visual aid to distinguish each team. Likewise, school uniforms can present a learning opportunity. With Bus-stop 2 Bus-stop™ educational uniforms and clothing, students can wear school uniforms with academic content to create style and **enhance** school culture.

A Low-Cost Educational Clothing Alternative

A cost effective alternative for schools with low budgets is to use embroidery, **adhesive** tags, or pin-on tags. Visitors should have academic content on their name tags. Cafeteria staff, janitorial staff, crossing guards, and maintenance crews should wear clothing with academic content also. This method of including academic content on clothing should include cheerleader uniforms, football jerseys, choir robes, and many other extra-curricular clothing. As role models, the school district and school administration personnel should also wear Bus-stop 2 Bus-stop™ clothing.

Testing Precautions and Other Concerns

Since Bus-stop 2 Bus-stop™ educational clothing features visual images of academic content, a plan should be created for district, state, and national testing. This educational clothing will need to be covered for the entire time span of the testing. A solution is for students to wear a regular school uniform or a temporary covering during any type of testing.

With new assessments such as the "Common Core State Standards," students are tested on a higher Depth of Knowledge (DOK) level. Although Bus-stop 2 Bus-stop™

educational clothing features basic concepts, the students will still have to apply them to answer a test question correctly. The following example shows an educational clothing item and one corresponding standardized test-type multiple choice question. As shown below, the student is still required to read (or listen) and apply his or her knowledge to answer the question.

Bus-stop 2 Bus-stop™ Clothing Example	Example Test Question
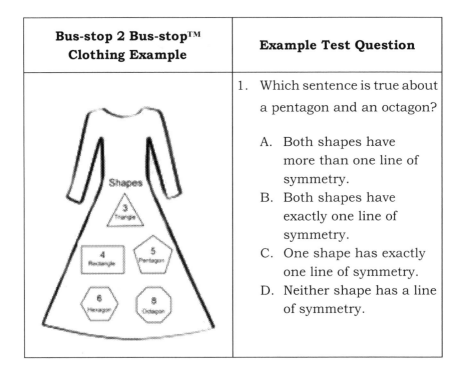	1. Which sentence is true about a pentagon and an octagon? A. Both shapes have more than one line of symmetry. B. Both shapes have exactly one line of symmetry. C. One shape has exactly one line of symmetry. D. Neither shape has a line of symmetry.

Information on Clothing and Society

Clothing plays an important role in American culture. Evidence from the earliest human civilizations proves the significance of clothing types. Factors such as climate, careers, religious beliefs, and geographical locations play a very large role in the physical appearance of certain clothing choices. The fabric, color, and style of a specific type of clothing often relates to one (or more) of the above factors. In America, the fashion industry is influenced by popular culture and forms of media. Modern trends sometimes stem from historical styles. American subcultures will take certain trends and eventually transform them into a lifestyle of specific clothing, as with sports uniforms. For example, ethnic clothing can tie into specific beliefs, religious values, or customs. Overall, global societies illustrate depth and diversity of clothing types in the world.

Clothing can be used to define a person's lifestyle and beliefs. Although the clothing worn may not reflect the person's individuality, it serves as a guide to initially judge a person. American society, through media and culture, has defined clothing types. Business wear, casual wear, swimwear, school uniforms, etc. can be used to identify, criticize, and categorize a person. Unlike cars, phones, or type of house, clothing criticism is usually taken very personally by the individual. Research points out a positive correlation between personal identity and clothing. Clothing is also capable of expressing personal thoughts and feelings. However, the interpretation of the clothing's visual appearance is up to a person's individual **perception**.

Many factors influence modern fashion today. The media and popular culture often influence new clothing fads and trends. Also, a person's environment and surroundings play a large role in influencing clothing styles and perceptions. Wealthy, middle class, and low class all differ in their perception of clothing types. For example, "wealthy" people do not consider cost, while "middle class" people wear clothing to satisfy the basic human need of warmth and protection, while still taking into account cost versus perception. Also, the weather affects a person's clothing. In fact, cold and snowy areas and hot tropical areas concentrate on their specific type of clothing to be marketed and sold in that area.

Discussion Questions for Chapter 7

1. In your opinion, will Bus-stop 2 Bus-stop™ clothing tags be more successful on school uniforms or casual clothing?
2. In your opinion, what is the best clothing item to display academic content on? (shirts, jackets, pants, hats, shoes, etc.) Why?
3. Should schools require students to wear educational clothing? Why or why not?
4. How does Dr. Gaines, the author of this workbook, feel about educational clothing? How do you know this?
5. According to the Chapter 7 information about clothing, what factors affect the physical appearance of clothing items?

Journal Activity for Chapter 7

Draw a picture of a t-shirt (or other clothing item) that displays academic content on the front. For this activity, create the t-shirt in a manner that will interest elementary children.

Write two paragraphs or more about your educational t-shirt and describe its appearance.

Vocabulary Word Review for Chapter 7

The following words were discussed in Chapter 7. On a separate sheet of paper, complete the following four steps for each word shown below.

- ✓ Write the word's definition (from a dictionary).
- ✓ Draw a picture to help you remember the word's meaning.
- ✓ Create a 2-3 word definition of the word.
- ✓ Write one or more sentences using the word.

perception	dissertation
adhesive	philosophy
enhance	appearance
diversity	standardized
atmosphere	embroidered

Fun Activity for Chapter 7

Create several outfits for a clothing line with academic content on the exterior (include shirt, skirt, socks, pants, shoes, hat, accessories). Use Dr. Gaines's clothing line as an example. Write an explanation about how the clothing could be used in a game or classroom lesson.

Scan this QR Code to read the press release about educational clothing.

Conclusion

So . . . Why are students not learning on the school bus and other non-traditional areas outside the classroom?

It would seem like the Bus-stop 2 Bus-stop™ method would have been created, implemented, and used in public schools a long, long time ago. After the U.S. released "A Nation at Risk" in 1983, American public schools were considered at-risk for future failure. At that point, authorities should have considered drastically restructuring public schools. Why did American school authorities decide to continue the same unsuccessful classroom practices without trying new out-of-the-classroom areas for learning?

Furthermore, mathematics and science achievement in America has steadily declined over the last two decades. National, state, and local school authorities have realized that solely learning inside the classroom is not working effectively. With technology and the Internet being updated at a fast changing pace, school districts must keep up with current trends. Schools should consider these updates and how to use this updated technology with the Bus-stop 2 Bus-stop™ method.

What do schools need to be successful with Bus-stop 2 Bus-stop™?

1. Clear educational goals and/or a mission statement
2. Policies and procedures that embrace the "Bus-stop 2 Bus-stop™" culture
3. Adaptation of this method to student's needs
4. High expectations for all students
5. Administer routine assessment
6. Provide multiple opportunities for Bus-stop 2 Bus-stop™ learning during the school day
7. Consider politics, ethics, and student safety while implementing this learning method
8. Make the Bus-stop 2 Bus-stop™ method relevant to students

Given the research findings and theories to aid in understanding failure of public schools in America, students should be learning academic content on the school bus. Actually, students should be learning academic content at the bus stop, cafeteria, playground, bathrooms, video arcades, and other areas of the school. The responsibility of student success falls upon the students, parents, teachers, and school administrators. Collaboratively, school staff members can analyze their school's culture and implement the Bus-stop 2 Bus-stop™ method based on individual student need. The future of education is looking much brighter with the Bus-stop 2 Bus-stop™ method for learning outside the classroom.

APPENDIX A

Social Clothing Line

Bus-stop 2 Bus-stop™ Clothing "makes learning stylish" with multiplication facts, with positive social meanings, on clothing items.

1's—Support/Learn about Groups of People		2's—Support/Learn about Volunteering	
1 x 1 = 1	Family/Family Reunion	2 x 1 = 2	Police/Fire Station
1 x 2 = 2	Friends	2 x 2 = 4	Animal Shelter
1 x 3 = 3	Church	2 x 3 = 6	Thrift Store
1 x 4 = 4	Sororities/ Fraternities	2 x 4 = 8	Library
		2 x 5 = 10	Community Clean Up
1 x 5 = 5	Siblings	2 x 6 = 12	Plant a Tree
1 x 6 = 6	Companies	2 x 7 = 14	Donate Time or Money
1 x 7 = 7	Professionals		
1 x 8 = 8	Legends	2 x 8 = 16	Soup Kitchen/ Food Bank
1 x 9 = 9	Celebrities	2 x 9 = 18	Local School
1 x 10 = 10	Brothers	2 x 10 = 20	Retirement/ Nursing Home
1 x 11 = 11	Sisters		
1 x 12 = 12	OTHER—Groups of People	2 x 11 = 22	Charity
		2 x 12 = 24	OTHER—Ways to Volunteer

3's—Support/Learn about the Military		4's—Support/Learn about Health/Medical Concerns	
3 x 1 = 3	Army	4 x 1 = 4	Cancer/ Breast
3 x 2 = 6	Army Reserve		Cancer
3 x 3 = 9	Army National	4 x 2 = 8	HIV/ AIDS
	Guard	4 x 3 = 12	Heart/ Kidney
3 x 4 = 12	Marine Corps		Disease
3 x 5 = 15	Marine Corps	4 x 4 = 16	Diabetes
	Reserve	4 x 5 = 20	Hypertension
3 x 6 = 18	Navy	4 x 6 = 24	Asthma
3 x 7 = 21	Navy Reserve	4 x 7 = 28	Stroke
3 x 8 = 24	Air Force	4 x 8 = 32	Injuries
3 x 9 = 27	Air Force Reserve	4 x 9 = 36	Alzheimer's Disease
3 x 10 = 30	Air National Guard	4 x 10 = 40	Learning/Mental
3 x 11 = 33	Coast Guard/ C. G.		Disability
	Reserve	4 x 11 = 44	Arthritis
3 x 12 = 36	OTHER—Military	4 x 12 = 48	OTHER—Health/ Medical
5's—Support/Learn about Sports		**6's—Support/Learn about the Environment**	
5 x 1 = 5	Hockey	6 x 1 = 6	Biodiversity
5 x 2 = 10	Golf	6 x 2 = 12	Nature Conservation
5 x 3 =15	Baseball	6 x 3 = 18	Global Warming
5 x 4 = 20	Soccer	6 x 4 = 24	Carbon Emissions
5 x 5 = 25	Martial Arts/Boxing	6 x 5 = 30	Natural Resources
5 x 6 = 30	Basketball	6 x 6 = 36	Natural Disasters
5 x 7 = 35	Motorsports	6 x 7 = 42	Recycling
5 x 8 = 40	Wrestling	6 x 8 = 48	Pollution Reduction
5 x 9 = 45	Football	6 x 9 =54	Save the Trees
5 x 10 = 50	Swimming	6 x 10 = 60	Clean Energy Sources
5 x 11 = 55	Tennis	6 x 11 = 66	Help Wildlife
5 x 12 = 60	OTHER—Sports	6 x 12 = 72	OTHER—Environment

7's—Support/Learn about Good Character		8's—Support/Learn about Popular Categories	
7 x 1 = 7	Love	8 x 1 = 8	Books
7 x 2 = 14	Peace	8 x 2 = 16	Technology
7 x 3 = 21	Self-Control	8 x 3 = 24	Fine Art
7 x 4 = 28	Creativity	8 x 4 = 32	Languages
7 x 5 = 35	Determination	8 x 5 = 40	History
7 x 6 = 42	Faith	8 x 6 = 48	Movies
7 x 7 = 49	Forgiveness	8 x 7 = 56	Music
7 x 8 = 56	Generosity	8 x 8 = 64	America
7 x 9 = 63	Loyalty/Obedience	8 x 9 = 72	Clothing
7 x 10 = 70	Patience	8 x 10 = 80	Video Games
7 x 11 = 77	Wisdom	8 x 11 = 88	Internet
7 x 12 = 84	OTHER—Good Character	8 x 12 = 96	OTHER—Popular Categories
9's—Support/Learn about Transportation		**10's—Support/Learn about U.S. Holidays**	
9 x 1 = 9	Cars	10 x 1 = 10	New Year's Day
9 x 2 = 18	Trucks/ SUV's	10 x 2 = 20	Memorial Day
9 x 3 = 27	Boats /Ships/ Submarines	10 x 3 = 30	Independence Day
		10 x 4 = 40	Labor Day
9 x 4 = 36	Motorcycles	10 x 5 = 50	Veteran's Day
9 x 5 = 45	Trains	10 x 6 = 60	Thanksgiving Day
9 x 6 = 54	Airplanes/ Helicopters	10 x 7 = 70	Valentine's Day
		10 x 8 = 80	Mother's Day
9 x 7 = 63	Bicycles/ Other Cycles	10 x 9 = 90	Father's Day
		10 x 10 = 100	Christmas Day
9 x 8 = 72	Buses	10 x 11 = 110	Halloween
9 x 9 = 81	Hot Air Balloon	10 x 12 = 120	OTHER—U.S. Holidays
9 x 10 = 90	Antique Vehicles		
9 x 11 = 99	Skateboard/ Snowboard		
9 x 12 = 108	OTHER— Transportation		

11's—Support/Learn about Animals		12's—Support/Learn about Education	
11 x 1 = 11	Dogs	12 x 1 = 12	Public Schools
11 x 2 = 22	Cats	12 x 2 = 24	Private Schools
11 x 3 = 33	Rodents	12 x 3 = 36	GED
11 x 4 = 44	Birds	12 x 4 = 48	High School Diploma
11 x 5 = 55	Reptile	12 x 5 = 60	Community College
11 x 6 = 66	Fish	12 x 6 = 72	4 year colleges/ universities
11 x 7 = 77	Frogs	12 x 7 = 84	Learning on the School Bus
11 x 8 = 88	Bugs		
11 x 9 = 99	Wildlife	12 x 8 = 96	Bus-stop 2 Bus-stop
11 x 10 = 110	Farm Animals	12 x 9 = 108	Dr. Keshia L. Gaines
11 x 11 = 121	Anti-Animal Cruelty	12 x 10 = 120	Vocational School
11 x 12 = 132	OTHER—Animals	12 x 11 = 132	Medical Doctor/ Ph.D.
		12 x 12 = 144	OTHER-Education

Appendix B

Information About the Original Book

Buy a Copy of the Original Book
"Why are Students Not Learning on the School Bus?"
www.iuniverse.com
www.amazon.com
www.barnesandnoble.com